BUILDING A LIFE WITH GOD

A STUDY FOR INDIVIDUALS AND GROUPS

By Jay R. Ashbaucher

Reid Ashbaucher Publications
Toledo, Ohio U.S.A.

REID ASHBAUCHER PUBLICATIONS
Toledo, Ohio U.S.A.
https://ra-publications.us

BUILDING A LIFE WITH GOD
A Study for Individuals and Groups
Copyright © 2020 by Jay R. Ashbaucher
All Rights Reserved

No part of this publication may be reproduced, stored in a retrieval system, or transmitted in any form or by any means electronic, mechanical, photocopying, recording, or otherwise, without the prior written permission of the author.

Scripture quotations taken from the New American Standard Bible® (NASB), Copyright © 1960, 1962, 1963, 1968, 1971, 1972, 1973, 1975, 1977, 1995 by The Lockman Foundation Used by permission. www.Lockman.org

Copyright © permissions can be obtained from the author through the following website: http://jay-ashbaucher.com

Cover image by Brian A. Jackson/Shutterstock.com

Library of Congress Control Number: 2020900233
Print ISBN: 978-1-7331399-2-2
eBook ISBN: 978-1-7331399-3-9

Printed in the United States of America
U.S. Printing History
First Edition: January 2020

Table of Contents

INTRODUCTION vii

1. USING METAPHORS 9
2. THE BEGINNING 15
3. THE GOAL 23
4. THE FOUNDATION 31
5. PUTTING THE PIECES TOGETHER 37
6. PERSEVERANCE 47

ABOUT THE AUTHOR 57

INTRODUCTION

My son was building a house. One day, as I was observing what he was doing, it occurred to me that building a house was like building a life with God; similar principles applied. I got the idea to use the house metaphor and metaphors in the Bible to help explain what building a life with God involves. Jesus often used metaphors to teach many of God's truths. For example, he used the metaphor of a "camel going through the eye of a needle" to emphasize how difficult it is for a rich person to enter the kingdom of heaven (Matthew 19:23-24). He used a farmer's seed to represent the word of God being sown in people's lives (Mark 4:14-15). He used bread to say he is the bread of life (John 6:48-51). In this study, we shall use Biblical metaphors as building blocks for building a life with God.

The first chapter is introductory and discusses God's use of three house metaphors to teach some of his truths. Each succeeding chapter represents another stage in the building process. When building a house, some preliminary things must be in place before we can successfully build, things like having a reason for building and making a plan. Knowing our goal and seeing what it will look like in the end certainly helps give us meaning, motivation, and a picture for what and how to build. Following those preliminary things, we start the actual construction work with a foundation. The foundation gives us a base to build upon before we gather and assemble all the parts needed to construct the house. The final chapter is all about perseverance, a necessary character quality if we are to finish well, for many discouraging problems are encountered along the way. All of these stages in building a house are involved in what it takes to build a meaningful life with God.

INTRODUCTION

Building a life with God is a lifelong process. Each of us has differing circumstances and issues that will determine at what rate, or how well we progress in our maturity as a follower of Christ Jesus. God is patient with each of us. We need to accept one another and help one another, remembering that we are all at a different place in our development as a Christian.

STUDY GUIDES AT THE END OF EACH CHAPTER
(For individuals or groups)

Suggestions for leading a group: These study guides lead deeper into the subject. If you are leading a group, depending on time and interest, you may want to choose which items to discuss. It is important, however, to look up and read the Bible verses, thinking about answering, and discussing each of the related questions. The questions are for self-discovery in learning about the scripture texts, and for promoting meaningful conversation.

You, or others, may have additional questions that arise. It is good to take time for these. If no one knows the answer, someone may research it and come back later with an answer. Also, if the group is led to discuss a matter that is off the topic, or expands the topic, and it seems meaningful to the members of the group, allow discussion to continue before coming back to the study. Because individuals can study on their own at home, you don't have to worry about finishing everything in the group meeting. Is it more important that the group enjoys each other and is having fun sharing and getting to know and love one another better, or that the group sticks to the study? Perhaps a balance of both is preferable.

CHAPTER 1

USING METAPHORS

I witnessed my son building a house. It is he and his wife's dream house being built on a beautiful location of their choice. It is not a large house, but he planned it in his mind, designed it, figured out much of the dimensional math, and sought help from engineers in how to construct it so it wouldn't fall down. He hired a contractor to give him counsel, provide contacts for ordering parts, make sure building codes were met, and to find tradesmen to build the parts he could not build himself. Using specific details, he recorded in his technical drawings, and with the help of a few families and friends, he built everything he could. I didn't have much to do with it, but I helped him in small ways, for example, one day I brought he and his helper lunch (wow, what a contribution). However, on another day, I helped him saw 4x8 plywood pieces that needed to be attached to his 40-foot steel I-beams (a little more helpful). Being a good father and fearing for his life, I did advise him to get a hard hat since he is doing all this dangerous construction, but at least he is using proper headgear when welding. I should also add that he encountered many unexpected and discouraging problems that hindered or delayed his progress along the way.

One day, as I watched all of this, I realized that building a life with God was a lot like building a house. Building a house is a good metaphor to help us understand what it takes to build a meaningful relationship with God. You may ask, "What is a metaphor?" A metaphor is a figure of speech used to compare one thing to another. Metaphors compare one thing to something else to help us better understand the something else.

For example, Jesus used metaphors to help explain the kingdom of heaven. He said, "The kingdom of heaven may be compared to a man who sowed good seed in his field" (Matthew 13:24), or "The kingdom of heaven is like a mustard seed" (Matthew 13:31), or "The kingdom of heaven is like a treasure hidden in the field" (Matthew 13:44). I am using a metaphor when I say building a life with God is like building a house.

Using a metaphor is good because it uses something we are familiar with, to help explain something that we are not as familiar with. We know from our experience something of what it means to build a house, and that helps us understand something we are not as familiar with, like building a life with God. So how does building a house help us understand what it takes and means to build a life with God? Let's begin by considering what it takes and what it means to build a house. We can then apply those things to what it takes and what it means to build a life with God.

God knows we all need a house of some kind. What is the purpose of having a house? One purpose is to have a place that protects us from many kinds of harmful weather conditions. Too much sun burns our skin and some of us can end up with a skin cancer. A house provides warmth in cold conditions. When there are windstorms and torrential rains, we are sheltered. Not only does a house protect us from harmful weather conditions, it also protects or shelters us from unwanted intruders. Some people rely on locked doors and security systems to help keep them safe. Although not completely guaranteed, a house also helps keep out bothersome bugs, also wild animals and bats, depending on where you live.

USING METAPHORS

Another purpose for a house is to provide a place where daily needs can be met. We can store food, prepare it, and serve meals. It provides a place to sleep and find needed rest. When we are sick or bodily injured, it is a place to stay while we recover. Not only is a house a shelter from dangerous elements, and a place to have our daily needs met, it is also a place where people are close together in proximity. This gives opportunity for them to know one another, to develop love for one another, and to influence each other's social, mental, emotional, and spiritual maturity; also, to prepare us for a future life. It is a place for fun, laughter, sadness, encouragement, learning, and correcting when we get off course. A place called home should be a place of peace, comfort, character building, and safety.

These same purposes for having a house apply to building a life with God. Building a life with God provides protection or shelter from dangerous elements that are all around us. We live in a dangerous world where evil lurks, seeking to lead us astray and destroy our well-being. Building a life with God meets many of our daily needs, and such a life brings us into proximity with a family that helps us grow to maturity. Furthermore, a life with God provides a home that gives us hope for a future that is better than any this world can give us.

How is a house built? It begins with an idea or felt need, including a goal and other preliminary preparations. When the actual building gets underway, a foundation is the first priority. The foundation is what the house is built upon and it needs to be solid or the house is susceptible to falling apart. After a solid foundation is established, other parts of the house can be built upon it. The house isn't completed all at once. There are many pieces that must be put together, and in a certain order.

Plumbing must go in, walls put in place, a roof put on, and so forth. When problems are encountered, perseverance is called for. There is also great satisfaction and joy as progress is made and completion is anticipated.

Likewise, building a life with God begins with felt needs, goals, and preliminary preparations. A solid foundation can then be built, followed by all the necessary pieces, all of which we shall discover in this study of Biblical metaphors. Building a life with God is not easy and does not happen all at once. We add pieces that lead to maturity as we live each day. We also meet with many hindrances and unexpected problems that slow us down and we must learn how to overcome them. God is preparing a house for us, and as we anticipate moving in, great joy is one of the rewards of building a life with God.

As we proceed with this study, we shall examine many biblical metaphors that help us understand what building a life with God involves. In future chapters we shall compare a life with God to familiar things like a soldier, a farmer, a rock, a door, a gift, the birth of a baby, the human body, a potter and clay, redemption, milk, ground drinking in the rain, and so forth. Examining these metaphors will help us better understand more about building a life with God. As I have an opportunity to talk with many Christians, and as I examine my own life, I find that we all have more to do in building our lives with God. Building a life with God is important, not only for ourselves, but so that others in need of faith, hope, and God's love, when they look at us, can see what God and a life with him looks like. As a human, Jesus built his life with God, others saw it, and many wanted to experience such a life.

STUDY GUIDE—GOING DEEPER

Following are three house metaphors used in Scripture. Read, think, and discuss the text and the questions.

House metaphor one: Read Hebrews 3:4-6. We are God's house. To be a house of God means he lives in us. He lives in us by the indwelling Christ, the Holy Spirit (Romans 8:9-11, 15-17). We are God's house in two ways: (1) As a body of God's people (1 Corinthians 3:9, 16-17) and (2) As individuals (1 Corinthians 6:19-20). Hebrews 3:6 says that Christ is "over his house." Discuss what that means, both for us as individuals, and for the church—Christ's body. Because Jesus lives in us by his Holy Spirit, what sort of people ought we to be? (To help answer this, you can refer to 1 Peter 2:5-17; also, 3:10-13) What helps us become the kind of person God wants us to be? (consider as part of your answer, Hebrews 10:24-25) Can you relate any personal stories of how someone helped you become a follower, or a better follower of Jesus?

House metaphor two: Read John 14:1-3. God's house has many rooms. Why would a person's heart be troubled? What does "to believe" in God and in Jesus mean? What does Jesus promise and when does it happen? Perhaps you can envision it by reading First Thessalonians 4:13-17.

House metaphor three: Read Psalm 127:1. Unless the Lord builds the house, we labor in vain. God built the earth to be our home (Genesis 1:26-2:1; 2:8). The earth is a biosphere—a sphere designed to sustain life. It has everything we need to sustain our physical lives. Humans created what they called biosphere 2. They attempted an enclosure that would duplicate earth and sustain people who lived inside it. It was an experiment to see if people could use it to live on another planet. People were closed in for two years to test it. For more info, you can google it. It failed for two reasons: (1) It failed to provide everything necessary for life to exist; it needed additional input from an outside source. (2) It failed because the people could not get along. It is an example showing that man alone cannot build a house like God can. They labored in vain when they tried. It takes the Lord to build a house that sustains life.

Discuss with one another: Why is it important to build a life with God? After discussing your answers, recall the reasons for building a house that were given in this chapter. Then, consider a few additional thoughts from the Bible on why it would be important for the Lord to build the house. What reasons can you find in the following passages (Mark 7:14-23; Psalm 119:50, 97-99; John 10:7-10; Hebrews 2:1-3)?

CHAPTER 2

THE BEGINNING

We are using a house metaphor and Biblical metaphors to help us understand what is involved in building a life with God. I realized something about my son's building of a house. Before he could build it, he needed an idea, a plan, and the ability to build it, otherwise, there would be no house. The same is true in building a life with God. Before we can do it, some preliminary things must be in place. Jesus uses a number of metaphors showing what needs to happen before we can successively build a life with God. These metaphors include conversion, a door, the birth of a baby, thirst-quenching water, and receiving a gift. Each metaphor contributes to a bigger picture of what is involved before beginning a life with God. Once we have what we need in order to build the house, we can set a goal, start the foundation, and build from there. Building a life with God has a preliminary beginning; otherwise, there is no life.

CONVERSION. In Matthew 18:3, Jesus says we must be converted. We know what conversion means. We can convert a piece of jewelry from a necklace into a ring. A convertible is a car that can be converted from having a rooftop to having the top down. Kids learn the meaning of converted through toys called transformers. A truck is converted into a different machine called a robot. To be converted means to change from one thing into another, like a worm into a butterfly. Building a life with God begins with a conversion. Conversion changes you in some way so that you now have what you need to build your life with God. According to Matthew 18:1-6, conversion changes us from living life our way, according to what we want, to being like a child who humbly believes in Jesus and wants to live life God's way.

A DOOR. Conversion is like going through a door, leaving one place and going into another. If I am outside a house, the proper way to get in is through a door. Likewise, the way into a relationship with God, and into his realm, is by entering through a door. Jesus uses the metaphor of a door. He said, "I am the door" (John 10:9). He is the doorway to a life with God. In other words, he is the one who makes it possible to come to God and to know him. He said, "No one comes to the Father, but through me" (John 14:6). Going through the door (Christ himself) leads to experiencing a life with God (Revelation 3:20).

BIRTH OF A BABY. Just as our physical life starts at our birth, so does our life with God. Jesus used the birth of a baby as a metaphor to help us see how life with God begins. Jesus said, "That which is born of flesh is flesh, and that which is born of Spirit is spirit. You must be born again (from above)" (John 3:6-7). "Unless one is born of water and the Spirit," he said, "one cannot enter the kingdom of God" (John 3:5). Even though people may disagree over the interpretation of the word water, Jesus is very clear that we need to be born from above by the Spirit of God. In other words, just as we are born into this world, and into a family, by a physical birth, we are born into God's world, and into his family, by a Spirit birth. This is a birth not caused by any human will or means, but a spiritual birth caused by God (John 1:13). Jesus said elsewhere, "It is the Spirit who gives life, the flesh profits nothing" (John 6:63). The Old Testament speaks of such a life in Ezekiel 36:25-27 where God says, "I will sprinkle clean water on you and you will be clean (from all your filthiness). Moreover, I will give you a new heart and put a new spirit within you. I will put my Spirit within you and cause you to walk in my statutes." We can successfully build a life with God when his Spirit has put God's eternal life into us and we are born into his family. The most important thing about this birth is receiving a new heart that enables us to want what God wants more than what we want.

THE GIFT OF LIVING WATER. Concerning this beginning of life with God, Jesus also uses the metaphors of a gift and living water. "If you knew the gift of God," he said to a woman, "you would have asked him, and he would have given you living water" (John 4:10). The woman Jesus talked to was thirsty, but he sensed that she needed to satisfy a thirst beyond drinking water. Having had five husbands and being yet in another relationship, apparently told Jesus that she was not finding what she was looking for, a relationship that would satisfy her deep felt need for love. Not knowing who Jesus was, or what he could offer her, she could not ask for what she needed. Jesus knew she was searching, and to meet her innermost needs he told her about a gift of living water that would quench her thirst for a satisfying life. We know what it means to receive a gift. A gift is something we can accept or refuse, but most often, we graciously receive it. A gift is not something we earn, but something we receive with thanksgiving. Sometimes, however, we do not get what we need unless we ask (see Luke 11:9-13).

What is living water, what has it to do with beginning a life with God, and how do we get it? Jesus offered living water to all people on an occasion when he taught in the temple in Jerusalem. On the last day of a feast, he cried out, "If anyone is thirsty, let him (or her) come to me and drink. The one who believes in me, from that person's innermost being will flow rivers of living water" (John 7:37-38). The scripture says that he was speaking of the Spirit, whom those who believed in him were to receive (John 7:39). Physically, we know water gives us life. If we do not get water, we die within a matter of days. The living water Jesus offers is himself, and those who have his Spirit in them will not die, but have an eternally satisfying life (1 John 5:11-12). According to John 1:12, we get life with God by believing in Jesus and by receiving him as the Lord of our life. This receiving is done by having faith in him and believing what he says. It's as if he is standing outside the door knocking and we open the door and invite him in. When we do this, he promises he will not reject us but give us life (John 6:37-40).

HOW IT WORKED IN MY LIFE. Jesus is the perfect model of Romans 10:14-15. He is the preacher of good news. Before we can believe and experience conversion, we need to hear God speaking to us in response to our felt needs. For example, one of my felt needs was the fear of dying. I needed to hear a message from God that I could have life and not die. The message someone shared with me from God's word was John 11:25-26, the one who believes in me will never die. Ephesians 1:13 says, "In Him, you also, after listening to the message of truth, the gospel of your salvation—having also believed, you were sealed in him with the Holy Spirit of promise." I found myself believing this good news. A peace came over me. Jesus promises his Spirit to all who believe. With his Spirit in us, our life will be different from what it was, taking us in new directions, with a new motivation, new desires, and his peace. Having been converted and born into God's family through faith in Jesus, and having received God's Spirit, we have a grateful and willing heart of love that leads us to want to build a life with God.

STUDY GUIDE—GOING DEEPER

How is Jesus the door to God? What did he do to make access to God possible? Discuss what the following words mean (you may need a dictionary). Pay particular attention to the results of what he did.

- A propitiation—1 John 2:1-2; 4:10
- A justifier—Romans 5:7-9
- A reconciler—Romans 5:10-11; 2 Corinthians 5:17-19; Colossians 1:20;
- A redeemer—Galatians 3:13-14; 4:4-5; Psalm 107:1-2
- A ransom—Matthew 20:28; 1 Timothy 2:5-6 (to free us from slavery - Hebrews 2:14-15);
- Our righteousness—1 Corinthians 1:30; Philippians 3:8-9
- He is the maker of our peace with God and each other—Romans 5:1; Ephesians 2:11-19.
- ***The conclusion Acts 4:12.

When we welcomed Jesus Christ to become our Savior and Lord, we have seen by the following scriptures that he came to dwell within us by his Spirit (Acts 2:16-17, 33; Romans 8:9-10; Galatians 3:13-14; Ephesians 1:13-14). Knowing that God's promised Spirit is living in us has far more impact on our lives than we often realize. In keeping with the words of Psalm 51:10, Ezekiel 36:25-27, and 2 Corinthians 5:17, can you explain how the Holy Spirit has changed your heart?

We do not always listen or heed the Spirit's voice within us. How can we practice the wisdom of Proverbs 4:23? (See for example Psalm 119:9-11).

Romans 8:11-27 records many blessings of the Spirit. These Scriptures identify how the Holy Spirit helps us in our daily lives. Read and discover how the Holy Spirit affects our future human bodies, our relationship to God, our fears, our hope in the midst of sufferings, our inheritance, and prayers for our well-being. Discuss what these blessings mean to you and how they have impacted your life.

I have heard some say they experience doubts that God is with and in them. They wonder if he is there for them, perhaps they feel abandoned by God in their time of need, or have not had answers to their prayers. How can we have assurance that God is living in us; that he is with us? How can we know? Consider a physical life as a metaphor. How do we know if our body is alive? There are signs that health professionals use, to see if we are alive. They check our pulse, respiration, pupils, brain waves, and so forth. In the letter from John (1 John), there are ways we know that we are spiritually alive. You can read through the letter and discover them for yourself. For example, how do you know God is in you according to 1 John 2:3-6 and 1 John 3:14-17? Do these things generally describe you? If needed, read through the book to discover other ways you know God is in you and you are spiritually alive.

CHAPTER 3

THE GOAL

As my son was working on his house, I realized that before building, something else was needed, something that inspired the building of the house. In his case, his whole building project was aimed at accomplishing a goal. He designed the house to meet his family's needs. Having the goal of providing for those he loves was a great motivator in working toward completing his house. This gave him purpose and meaning in what he was doing. With a purpose and a goal in mind, the building takes shape as the builder knows what to build. In the same way, understanding the goal for building a life with God enables us to know where we are headed, and motivates us to press on to reach it.

The Bible uses the metaphor of running a race to help us understand the importance of having a goal (1 Corinthians 9:24-27). Athletes who run races have a track or path to run on and they have a finish line they are aiming to reach. The goal is to stay on course, and to run in such a way as to win the race. The apostle Paul uses this metaphor to remind us that it is keeping our eyes on the goal that determines the preparation and work it takes to cross the finish line. Running a race is not just a physical effort, we must pay attention to our inner self, just as the runner of a race pays attention to whatever it takes within him or herself to win the race. It takes planning, knowledge, discipline, and wisdom to run a good race and finish well. Building a life with God also has a finish line. Knowing our goal determines how we build. What is the goal God has for us? What are we aiming at?

Our goal is twofold, there is both a present and a future goal. Actually, the goal to cross the finish line includes multiple goals. The Bible identifies three present goals, though there are certainly more we could add. The first present goal is in Romans 8:29. This goal is to become more like Christ. A second goal is clear, 1 Timothy 1:5 and Ephesians 3:17 tells us our goal is to love from a pure heart. Third, through becoming like Jesus and learning to love as he loves us, we are to be involved in making disciples, that is, helping others to become followers of Jesus (Matthew 28:19-20).

Beyond these immediate or present goals, the future goal, also including many parts, is to attain the prize spoken of by the apostle Paul. Our present goals lead to attaining the ultimate prize—our future inheritance (Philippians 3:14). Just as humans, in this present world, leave an inheritance for their kids (Proverbs 13:22), so God, in his future world, has an inheritance for his children (Acts 20:32). The metaphor of being heirs to an inheritance, passed on to us from our parents, is likened to our receiving an inheritance from God our Father. What is it we are to inherit? Our all-encompassing inheritance is eternal life—we shall not die, but be raised from the dead and live with God in an evil free world that will last forever (Romans 8:15-25; John 3:16; 11:25-26; 1 Corinthians 6:14; Revelation 21:1-7). Eternal life offers many other things that we can look forward to, such as, a new heaven and a new earth, a resurrected body, and no more pain or sorrow. Jesus promised a number of future blessings that his people would one day experience because of their life with him. They would be comforted from their grief, inherit the earth, reach a longed-for perfection and righteousness, see God, and possess the kingdom of heaven (Matthew 5:3-10).

THE GOAL

These and other promises of God make up what we call "our hope." Hope, in our human thinking, means wishful thinking. We hope something will happen, for example, we hope it will not rain Saturday so we can go on our outing, or we hope things will work out in our troubled family life. This meaning of hope believes that things we want could happen, but they are not for certain, we must wait and see. Christian hope is based on what we know will happen, we can count on it because God can and will make it happen. Abraham, the father of our faith, saw God's goal as his hope, and it motivated him to keep believing, growing in his life with God, and staying faithful to God (Hebrews 11:8-10, 13-19). Not only would he enjoy a future home in heaven, he also knew by faith that he would inherit the world (Romans 4:13).

Hope of what is coming comforts us. It encourages us to keep pressing on to reach it. Part of what comforts believers is Jesus's coming again to make all things right, and even though we may die before that happens, our hope involves being together again with believing loved ones, and with our loving Lord, in his glorious kingdom (1 Thessalonians 4:13-18). The apostle Paul runs the race, keeping his eye, not only on the present goals, but on a future life with God, and that is why he says, "I press on so that I may lay hold of that for which I was also laid hold of by Christ Jesus." It is keeping his eye on the goal that motivates the apostle Paul to press on with his life, even in the midst of great difficulties and sufferings (Philippians 3:7-21). He presses on in a way that will enable him to cross the finish line and gain the prize.

Our goal, as stated in Hebrews 6:1, is the goal of aiming to gain maturity in our life with God. Maturity means being perfect as God is perfect (Matthew 5:48), holy as God is holy (1 Peter 1:15-16), and pure as he is pure (1 John 3:2-3). Like Paul, we have not reached perfection, but we continually move toward it because we know that our ultimate goal of perfection in a perfect world will be our prize in the end. Remember, we cannot do this alone. This is why the preliminary essentials to a life with God discussed in chapter two of this book is necessary. We must have God dwelling in us by his Holy Spirit. The Spirit is our promised helper (John 14:16-17; Acts 1:4-5; 2:38-39; 11:15-17). With God's help, the goals of a life with God can be attained.

In the movie, The Hobbit, Bilbo and his dwarf friends were headed for the dwarves' homeland, which had been taken from them. They had to go through a forest to get there and in the forest, they became disoriented, lost, depressed, and faced many dangers that were preventing them from reaching their destination. Bilbo got the idea to climb a tree to rediscover their bearings. From above the forest he could see the mountain that was home to the dwarves. He climbed down and said he knew the way. With renewed hope and strength, they aimed in that direction and faithfully pressed on with greater determination to reach their goal. We may have a goal, but unless we continually see where we are supposed to be headed, we can become sidetracked or lost, and not know how to get there.

STUDY GUIDE—GOING DEEPER

This diagram helps us visualize the goal we must keep in mind in order to build a life with God. We keep our mind and heart on the goal, or we get off track.

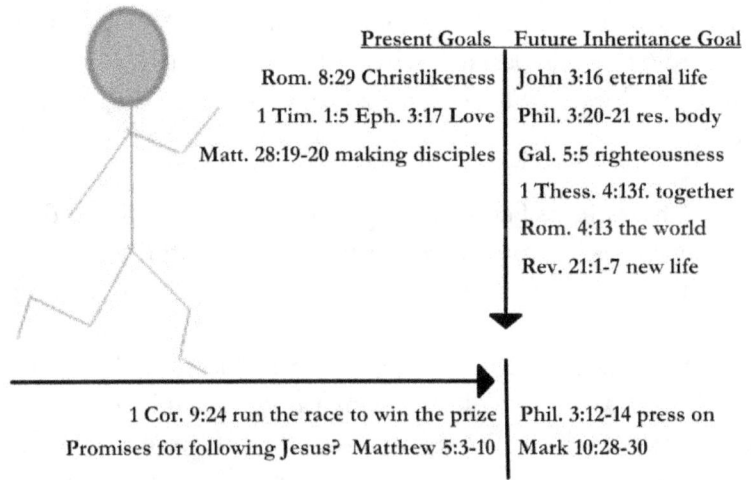

Since Christlikeness is a goal, we need to know, what is Christlike? Jesus is our Teacher and our Lord (John 13:13). One day he humbled himself before his disciples (the word disciple means "learner"). He washed their feet (John 13:5). Then he said, "Do you know what I have done to you?" (John 13:12) Then he answered the question by saying, "I gave you an example that you should do as I did to you" (John 13:15). How would you explain what Jesus meant? What example did he set for us? How are we to be like him?

It seems there is within us humans a desire to put ourselves above others, to be recognized and esteemed in the eyes of others, to enjoy a position of authority. No doubt, there is some validity to this because we are to be responsible for the welfare of others and are put in certain positions to be over them. What positions of authority has God given you to fulfill in your life? What does your position of authority require that you do? We all have a certain position or degree of authority, but how does God want us to use our authority? Study Matthew 20:24-28. According to this passage, what is Jesus teaching his disciples and why does he find it necessary to teach this? From these scriptures, what do we learn about what Jesus is like?

What is Jesus like according to John 15:12-13? What does lay down our life for others mean? According to these verses, how are we to be like Jesus?

Not only is one of our goals to press on to be like Jesus, but in doing so, difficult problems can occur and we become discouraged. Can you share about a time you were attempting to accomplish something and what it was that caused you to become discouraged? What does Second Corinthians 4:16-18 say to us that will encourage us? How does First Corinthians 15:58 encourage us? How is building a life with God the work of the Lord? Why do you know that what you are doing is not in vain?

When my son was building his house, he frequently had to look at his plan to see what he was building. He must keep seeing what the goal looks like if he wants the house to end up as intended and meet his family's needs. As you review the diagram above, remember the goal God has set before you. The goal is so fantastic, it is worth every effort to reach it (1

Corinthians 15:58). With God's help (John 15:5), keep running to gain the prize.

CHAPTER 4

THE FOUNDATION

My son is building a house for his family. That is his primary goal. Therefore, the house has been designed to meet his family's needs, as well as to fulfill some of their desires. Likewise, God is building a house for his family. He too builds it to meet his family's needs and longings. It was time for my son to build the house's foundation. His foundation had to take into account, not only basic materials such as concrete and rebar but also, additional items that would meet particular needs of the people living in the house, for example, electricity, water, and drainage. Furthermore, the type of land on which my son built his house required that workers pound steel pillars into the ground to ensure the house is built on solid rock. God's house also needs a solid foundation lest it crumble under stress. We shall use Biblical metaphors of a rock and a house foundation to help us know the right foundation on which to build our life with God.

We begin with the rock metaphor. Jesus asked his disciples, "Who do you say that I am?" Simon Peter answered, "You are the Christ (Messiah), the Son of the living God." Jesus said to Simon, "You are Peter and upon this rock I will build my church, and the gates of Hades will not overpower it" (Matthew 16:15-18). The word rock is a metaphor, a figure of speech for the foundation upon which Jesus wants to build his people. What is the rock?

There have been three primary ideas of what Jesus, in Matthew 16:18, means by the word, rock: (1) Peter is the rock,

(2) Peter's confession of faith in Jesus is the rock, and (3) Jesus is the rock. People tend to limit the interpretation of the rock to only one of these three, and they argue over which one. All three make sense to me, but you can decide for yourself whether you think all three meanings are true.

First, it cannot be denied that Jesus says Peter is the rock. The name, Peter, means a rock or stone, and on Peter, Jesus will build his church. Jesus gave him that name when he first met him, using the Aramaic word (Cephas), meaning rock or stone (John 1:42). When you read in the book of Acts the story of how the church had its start, you will see how Peter's strong leading role was foundational for establishing Christ's church (read for example Acts 1:15; 2:14; 4:8; 8:14-17; 10:1-5, 11:13-18). What Peter did was certainly instrumental in laying the foundation for the building and expanding of God's kingdom to include both Jews and Gentiles. Additionally, Peter's influence in the lives of God's people continues to this day through his written reminders of the Lord's truths (2 Peter 1:12-15; 3:1-2).

What made Peter a rock? He was a person who, with God's help, knew without a doubt who Jesus was, and by his confession of faith, he revealed the identity of Jesus to others. Peter did not point to himself, but to Jesus as the one everyone needed to rely on. According to Peter, Jesus is truly the ultimate foundation of our faith, being the corner stone (see 1 Peter 2:6). To this fact, the scriptures agree (Psalm 118:22). Furthermore, Jesus is the author, finisher, and chief example of our faith (Hebrews 12:2). The scripture also says, "For no man can lay a foundation other than the one which is laid, which is Jesus Christ." Peter, along with all the apostles and prophets are

THE FOUNDATION

God's fellow workers, helping to lay that foundation. You and I, who have believed the apostles and prophets testimonies concerning Jesus, are God's building (see 1 Corinthians 3:9-11). We are of God's household, *built on the foundation of the apostles and prophets* (emphasis added), Christ Jesus himself being the one in whom we are being built together into a dwelling of God in the Spirit (Ephesians 2:19-22). Peter and the other apostles experienced life with Jesus and taught people the truth about Jesus. The word of God came to them and they passed those truths on to us (1 John 1:1-3). Peter certainly had an important part in the founding of the church of Jesus Christ, but he definitely pointed away from himself to Jesus as the foundation on which we build. Additionally, Peter's confession of faith in who Jesus was is the same faith we also must have (2 Peter 1:1).

Besides a rock, Jesus used the metaphor of a house foundation in Matthew 7:24-27. All who build their house on a rock, that is, who build their life on a solid foundation, do so when they listen to Jesus's words and do what he says. The teachings of Jesus and God's word are the foundation on which we build a life with God. In another scripture, it is said this way, "We are like a man building a house, who dug deep and laid a foundation upon the rock; and when a flood occurred, the torrent burst against that house and could not shake it, because it had been built well" (Luke 6:48). Being well built and unshakable is what we are when we build our life on the solid rock, which is Jesus and his word (Luke 6:47).

An example of the importance of building our lives on God's word is seen when we read about the Israelites in the Old Testament. Through Jeremiah, God warned his people that their lives were in danger of falling into ruin. The reason given for their lives falling into ruin was their refusal to listen to the word of God and do what he said (see Jeremiah 16:10-13; 18:10-12; 25:3-11). Why is God upset with his people and treating them this way? We must remember that God chose Israel to represent him to all the peoples of the earth. They are not fulfilling what God wanted them to do. Instead of representing God to the nations, they are joining the nations and worshipping those nations' gods. We are not only called to build our lives on Jesus and his word for our own personal benefit, but because we are representatives of Jesus and God's salvation to others around us, so that they too can believe and enjoy the salvation of God (Matthew 28:18-20). Building a life with God is important to him because we are his people chosen to help others come to know God.

What Peter and the other apostles and prophets witness, believe, and confess concerning Jesus, and what they pass on to us in their teachings from God's word, is what forms the foundation for building a life with God. Peter is a key contributor (see 2 Peter 1:1-21). We can thus conclude that the following four things form the foundation on which to build a life with God: Peter's role (along with the other prophets and apostles), knowing Jesus personally, having undying faith in Jesus, and obeying the teachings of Jesus. Our answer to Jesus's question, "Who do you say that I am?" is the start of determining weather, or not, we are building our life with God on a solid foundation. What do you believe about Jesus, and why?

STUDY GUIDE—GOING DEEPER

1. From where have you gotten your information about Jesus? Are these reliable sources? Why or why not?

2. As an individual or group, name the things you believe about Jesus, and then explain why you believe them.

3. Simply having information about Jesus does not mean a person believes in him or trusts him. The devil believes things about Jesus, but is not a believer as others are. How would you explain the difference between knowing about Jesus and having a personal relationship with him?

4. Life is not easy. Things happen that can emotionally be very unsettling. If you are a Christian seeking to build a life with God, what is the foundation that holds you up, strengthens you, and keeps you from falling apart. Explain how it works for you. My 5-year-old grandson was once extremely frightened by a big dog that was approaching him. He ran screaming into the arms of his father. How do you think my grandson felt when with his dad? We are offered a similar safe place. How can Proverbs 18:10 be foundational in our own lives when bad things happen?

5. Read Genesis 12:2-3; 18:17-18; 22:15-18; 26:1-5; 28:10-14. What does God promise Abraham and his descendants? What role are they to have toward other nations and people of the world? In the New Testament, Peter preached to the people the message that Christ has come to save them (read Acts 3:11-26). Peter reminded them that this was a fulfillment of what had been promised long ago, that through God's people, the Jews,

he would bless the nations of the world (Acts 3:25). It is the gospel of Jesus that God had in mind when he chose Israel to bless all the nations (see Galatians 3:8).

6. Read First Peter 2:9-12. Israel failed to fulfill one of God's key purposes for their lives. At the present time, the people of Christ's church are called to do it. Who does God say we are in verses 9-10? What would you say is the job of a priest of God? Why would you say God calls us a holy nation? What is the reason God has chosen us according to verse 9? In verses 11-12, what words describe us? How do these verses say we are to live—what are we to be doing? How would you define "excellent behavior" in the midst of an unbelieving world? How can we be expected to be treated if we take a stand for Jesus in our day and age? Verse 12 mentions "good deeds." What good deeds are we doing, both individually, and as a church?

7. According to Romans 12:21, what is a primary purpose of good deeds? What example is given in Romans 12:20? In Titus, good deeds are mentioned six times. Read the following verses and discuss what each one says about good deeds, Titus 1:16; 2:7, 14; 3:1, 8, 14. How can we recognize pressing needs in our daily normal routines? We often have opportunities to surprise people with acts of kindness in our daily situations. Share any good deeds you have witnessed or been involved with in your daily walk with God. Here are other scriptures that talk about good deeds if you care to look them up (Philemon 1:14; Acts 10:38; 1 Peter 3:8-13; 3 John 11; Isaiah 1:16-17).

CHAPTER 5

PUTTING THE PIECES TOGETHER

In chapter 5 we shall discuss some important pieces that need to be gathered and put together to build our life with God. Before my son built his house, he formed an idea of what he wanted and needed for his family. He put his ideas on paper and was able to draw a picture of what the finished house would look like. Of course, he had to formulate a list of all the materials he would need to build the house. He made drawings of how to put the pieces together so the house would look like the picture. Furthermore, he needed to know what tools and skills and outside help would be needed to construct it.

Likewise, when we build a life with God, God gives us a picture of what the finished product looks like. Having been made in God's image, we are to look like him. We are to be perfect as he is perfect (Matthew 5:48), and pure and holy as he is pure and holy (1 John 3:2-3; 1 Peter 1:15-16). Building a life with God means to put the pieces together that will conform us, little by little, into the image of God. Jesus is our model of a human who is the perfect image of what God is like. It is said of Jesus that he is an exact representation of the nature of God (Hebrews 1:3). He made the claim that anyone who sees him has seen the Father (John 14:8-9). Knowing what we are to look like, we gather all the pieces together and construct our life to look like the picture God gave us, the person of Jesus. (Romans 8:29). The following metaphors let us know some pieces we need in order to build a life with God.

1. A VINE AND BRANCHES (John 15:4-5). In this metaphor, the vine produces the nutrients needed to feed the branch so that the branch can produce the fruit intended by its creator. For example, a branch cannot produce a grape if it is separated from the vine. It can do nothing without remaining connected to the vine and receiving all that the vine feeds into it. Jesus is the vine and we are the branches. We have already seen that Jesus, our faith in him, and doing what he says, is the foundation on which we build. As the branch relies on the vine for what it needs to grow the fruit, so we rely on Jesus to provide what we need in order to build a life with God. Remaining in Jesus means to trust him completely. Jesus knows the plans he has for us. We must believe that his plans are accurate and follow those plans if we want his house to be completed as he intends. Without him, we cannot do it (Psalm 127:1).

2. WALKING (Ephesians 4:1). Jesus healed people who were lame, crippled, or could not walk. We are all crippled in some way, whether physically, mentally, socially, or morally. Walking is important to us if we are to get around in life and do things we love doing. A house could not be built if the builders could not walk from place to place to perform their tasks. The Bible often uses the metaphor of walking to describe building a life with God. Here are a few examples that define how a Christ-follower is to walk. In Ephesians 4:1-3, 17-19 we are to walk in a manner worthy of his calling. It is a calling to a mature love, not to living in the darkened and ignorant way of our former life (Ephesians 5:7-15). In Romans 6:4 we are to walk in newness of life. This involves realizing the death of our old self and letting our new resurrected self be in control. In Galatians 5:25 we are to walk by the Spirit of God. In 2 Corinthians 5:7

we are encouraged to walk by faith and not by sight. Walking with Jesus means to live continually in his powerful presence, applying his teachings to our daily life.

3. POTTER AND CLAY (Isaiah 64:8). This metaphor is about persons who form objects made of clay into vessels of their choosing. God the Father, through Jesus and His Spirit, is our creator and we voluntarily allow him to build us according to his plans (Isaiah 29:16; 45:9-10; Psalm 139:13-18; Revelation 21:4-5). Just as a house is formed by those who trust the builder's plans, so a believer is formed by trusting the plans of God. Many fear this, they fear giving control of their lives into the hands of another. But God has good plans for us. We need not fear his ways and promised good for our future. We may suffer in this evil world, but the Lord is taking us out of it, promising to make us new and perfect and whole.

4. REST (Isaiah 30:15). My son at times would say that work on the house made him tired. Without rest we are subject to frustrations, confused thinking, and mistakes. Jesus grew weary from his life's journey and needed to rest. He often went aside to pray and regain strength and perspective on his personal life and work (Matthew 14:23; Luke 6:12). We are invited to come to him when we need rest (Matthew 11:28-30). God promises to give strength to the weary (Isaiah 40:29-31).

5. ELEMENTARY TEACHINGS; DRINKING MILK (Hebrews 6:1-2; 1 Corinthians 3:1-3). Building a house requires continual learning and new skills. As my son began to build his house, he had a basic understanding of how to use his tools, but as he continued to build, he needed to consult with others on what to do. He learned more and gained more skills as he went

along. We start out drinking milk as infants, but we must progress to solid foods. We start with elementary basics in school and progress to greater understandings and maturity. In Hebrews 6 and First Corinthians 3, we are told to receive and be grounded in those basic understandings of our faith, but not to stay there. Maturity comes with greater knowledge and experience in living that out. Maturity is looking more and more like Jesus by loving as he loved and doing good in the world around us as he did good (John 13:34; Acts 10:38; Galatians 6:9-10).

6. THE HUMAN BODY (1 Corinthians 12). The metaphor of our human body shows us that many parts, large and small, are needed to have a body that functions well. Each part is important because it contributes something that the body needs. My son did not know everything about building a house, nor did he have the experience, tools, or skills to do some of the work. He relied on others to help him. Many people loaned him things like scaffolding and a metal-folding machine, things that were needed to be able to complete the building. In building a life with God we need to be part of a body that supplies things we need to complete us. That body is made up of other believers who possess gifts we are to receive so that we can mature in Christ (Ephesians 4:11-16). We are encouraged to meet together faithfully, to build one another up, stimulating one another to love and good deeds (Hebrews 10:24-25).

Of course, we know that building a life with God on our own is humanly impossible. We need a savior who makes it possible. First, we need to understand that in God's mind, the finished product is already done. To God, because of our faith in Jesus, we are already declared justified and righteous in God's sight (Romans 5:1; Galatians 2:16; 3:6-9). However, while on the earth, we are not perfect and are called to build our lives in that direction. As we build, we must always keep the finished product in mind so we stay on course and don't get discouraged. As in building a house, we will encounter problems and make mistakes that hinder our progress. Keeping the goal of Christlikeness in mind, and receiving forgiveness by God (1 John 1:9), enables us to make corrections and keep moving ahead toward the finish line.

STUDY GUIDE—GOING DEEPER

There are many materials to gather that help us build a life with God. The kinds of materials we use determine our success (see 1 Corinthians 3:9-15). Our building starts with receiving Jesus and learning essential elementary things, basic teachings of the faith. From there, we build little by little, piece by piece, until he comes, and the house is finally completed according to God's plan. The apostle Paul encourages us with these words, "I am confident of this very thing, that he who began a good work in you will perfect it until the day of Christ Jesus (Philippians 1:6). Following are additional metaphors; building blocks to add to our materials list.

Fire (James 3:5-10). The metaphor of fire is used to teach about our tongues. How is our tongue compared to a fire? Why is our speech so hard to control?

Taste (Psalm 34:8). Can you identify ways you have tasted God's goodness? According to Luke 17:11-19, what does Jesus expect from those who experience God's goodness?

To say that God is the potter and we are the clay is to allow God to be the loving boss of our lives. Consider parents and children (Ephesians 6:1-4). Assuming parents are following the Lord's ways, if the children refuse to obey them, they are in danger of being separated from the authority that enables them to grow to be good people as God wants them to be. Consider a man and woman in marriage. As imperfect people, they can expect differences. It is common that they have difficulties getting along and are at odds with each other. They are in danger of divorce. But what if each one allowed Jesus to be the boss? How would that change how they relate in love and respect toward one another (Ephesians 5:33)?

According to Hebrews 6:4-5, how would you explain the things from God that we have tasted? What warning is given in Hebrews 6:6-8? In spite of this warning, what encouragement do we have in verse 9? What do you think are the "better things" referred to in this verse? (Do verses 10-12 supply us with an answer to the "better things" the writer of verse 9 has in mind) What do these verses (10-12) tell us we are to do? What do they say we are to believe? How would you define the promises and hope we have?

Ground that drinks the rain (notice this metaphor in Hebrews 6:7-8). We are like ground that drinks the rain. When rain falls on the planted crops, they bring forth vegetation. Some ground, however, does not produce the vegetation intended. Instead of useful crops that bless us, we end up with thorns and thistles. How is that possible? Perhaps the reason for bad crops is not the rain, but the ground on which the rain falls.

Jesus told a story about seed sown in the ground (Mark 4:1-8). What is the seed? The seed was meant to produce a good crop, a crop that would bless people. The problem was not with the seed, but with the ground (Mark 4:14-20). The ground represents four kinds of people on whom the seed is sown (or we might say, the ground on which the rain falls). What determines what kind of vegetation, or fruit, the crop produces? How are the four persons described in this story? How would you describe your present life? If you are not satisfied with your life, and you want to produce the kind of life God wants for you, knowing about these four soils, what changes would you need to make?

CHAPTER 6

PERSEVERANCE

Perseverance means to keep doing something in spite of problems or difficulties. Perseverance means to continue to fulfill your purpose faithfully; you don't quit. As my son was building his house he ran into many problems along the way, some of them hindered his progress and were quite discouraging. Problems encountered included materials not delivered at the time he needed them, and sometimes the wrong parts came, for example, when he got a shipment of floor joists instead of roof joists. Mistakes he or manufacturers made often required time-consuming correction. Defective parts needed to be sent back, or bad weather caused him to lose many days of work. Some days he felt sore and tired and preferred not to keep going. Sometimes there were interruptions that needed attention, drawing him away from his task. As winter approached, snow came, and it became more urgent to get the house enclosed. He needed encouragement along the way to help him persevere.

Something else requires perseverance. We must build in a world that is decaying and dying. Not only are there many things that must be overcome if our building is to be completed, but once we think it is finished, we encounter the second law of thermodynamics. This law states that things in our world are in a state of decline, that is, losing energy or falling apart, and they cannot hold together without continued maintenance and repair. It seems true that, in an imperfect world, we can never stop persevering if we want to build a house, or a life, that lasts.

We are going to face hard things (2 Thessalonians 1:3-5; Revelation 14:9-12). Jesus said we would have troubles and persecutions in this world (John 16:33; Mark 10:30). The good news is, unlike this world, God's future world for us will never fall apart. But for now, there is the need for us to overcome our imperfections and problems and keep going if we want to achieve the kind of life God promises us. Although my son found himself frequently working alone, there were many times when family and friends showed up to help. Fortunately, in building a life with God we can be encouraged because others are there to help us, especially God, who gives us strength and promises to complete what he has planned for us. His plan is for us to one day be living in his house and enjoying a forever peaceful and satisfying life that is free of all evils and problems. But to get there requires that we persevere (Romans 5:3-4). Jesus needed to persevere (Hebrews 12:1-2). As the apostle Paul said, "I press on toward the goal for the prize of the upward (earth-lived and heaven-bound) call of God in Christ Jesus" (Philippians 3:14).

The life of a soldier (2 Timothy 2:3-4) is one metaphor used to represent perseverance. The things they must suffer through are hard and there are times they want to leave, but can't. The soldier realizes he or she is in active service to the country and government that has enlisted him or her. No soldier in active service entangles him or herself in the affairs of everyday life. They are devoted to pleasing the ones who are over them and they must push through whatever obstacles are before them, whether tough training or engagement in dangerous battles. The weapons of a soldier's warfare provide us with a metaphor to help us understand what we need to overcome tough times (Ephesians 6:10-18). To ward off the attacks against us, there is self-protective armor to put on, plus, offensive weapons we must use to defeat the things that come against us.

Two other metaphors that encourage us to persevere are those of an athlete and a farmer. The first metaphor, the athlete (2 Timothy 2:5), must engage in disciplined training and follow the rules required in running the race. "Discipline yourself for the purpose of godliness" says Paul in First Timothy 4:7-10 (see also Hebrews 12:1-13 for God's training method). Through perseverance, we will gain benefits, both for this life, and for the life to come.

The second metaphor is the farmer (2 Timothy 2:6). The farmer works hard at plowing, planting, and taking care of his crop so that he and his family receive what is needed to sustain their lives. He knows there are lots of ways his crop could fail, but he also knows that if he doesn't keep going, he will get no crop at all. Faith and hope help's him persevere. In a Nanny McPhee movie, a farmer's wife struggles to keep the farm going and must get the crop in or possibly lose the farm. She works hard and stays the course because her husband is off at war and she wants the farm to be there when he gets back. One day she receives word that he was killed in action. She loses what she hoped for, loses her motivation to persevere, and prepares to sell the farm. Fortunately, others help her to hang on, and shortly thereafter, her husband surprisingly shows up. She was glad she did not quit. How important is hope as a motivator to keep persevering?

We need continual reminders to know why we persevere. It is to receive the prize—to reach the goal of building a successful life with God (see 2 Timothy 2:8-13). Writers of the Bible give us frequent reminders to help us keep going. Paul emphasizes the importance of reminding (2 Timothy 1:6; 2:14). Peter does the same. He says, "I stir you up by way of reminder" (2 Peter 1:12-15; also 3:1). John writes to believers, not because they do not know things; they do know. We tend to forget; therefore, he reminds them of God's truths (1 John 2:20-21). In addition, we can help ourselves, and others, by persevering in prayer for each other (Ephesians 6:18). We also have our family of believers to encourage us and help us to persevere (Hebrews 10:24-25).

If you read both of Paul's letters to Timothy, you will discover many words that describe persevering. I will mention most of them and you can read the letters for yourself to discover what problematic situations perseverance will overcome. Words Paul uses to encourage us to persevere in building a life with God include the following: guard, endure, fight the good fight, continue, retain the standard, be convinced, be strong, be diligent, suffer hardship, rely on God, keep free from sin, take care, discipline yourself, and keep the goal in mind.

Let us remember that as believers, we are citizens of a country different from any other in this world. We are citizens of the kingdom of God (1 Peter 2:9-10). In that country, we have a king who rules with love and good will for all his subjects. Building a life with God is more important than anything else we could ever achieve. God's promised rewards will never fail us because God has the power to fulfill every one of them. Furthermore, do not forget, he intends for his kingdom to come on earth as it is in heaven. Therefore, we care about all the peoples of this earth, that through the good we do, and the message of God we share, we are helping to build, not only our own lives, but God's kingdom of love that exists to include all peoples of the earth (Revelation 5:9-10). We are building a life with God so that, as God's co-workers, we can be part of bringing his kingdom on earth as it is in heaven (Matthew 6:9-10).

STUDY GUIDE–GOING DEEPER

In Hebrews 12:1-13, we learn some things that help us to run with endurance, to persevere. As you read this passage, can you find at least 5 reasons that cause us to lose our perseverance and get off course from attaining our goal? Explain why Jesus was able to endure the cross (12:2)? In 12:5-13, how does discipline help us to be able to persevere through trials? According to these verses, why is discipline hard to take? What do these verses say we must do in order for discipline to help us? In these verses, what is the result of being disciplined? What are some ways you think God disciplines us?

Sometimes, when things are not working out well for us, God seems absent, and we are tempted to think God has abandoned us and that he does not care. On YouTube, in a Messenger Studios short movie called Abandoned, a girl loses her sight and thinks her loving father has abandoned her. The movie illustrates how God may work in our lives in ways we do not see or expect. We think he is not helping us, but all the time he is there. He has withdrawn himself from our view to help us grow strong and better be able to handle life's problems. How is God helping us grow stronger when we think he has left us? Why do you think God wants us to be strong apart from him? On the other hand, why do we need him?

Read 2 Kings 6:15-17. In this context, an enemy army had surrounded the city where Elisha was staying and their objective was to capture him. Verse 15 begins with Elisha's servant discovering this very unsettling danger. How would you describe this servant? Why does Elisha tell his servant not to fear and what does Elisha pray for his servant? When we have a problem and God seems absent, how can we apply principles in this passage to our own lives? In another place in the Bible, Joshua is to lead God's people into their Promised Land. There will be difficulties and battles to face. What words does Moses give to the people to encourage them (Deuteronomy 31:6)? How does Moses encourage Joshua (Deuteronomy 31:7-8)? If there are times you think God does not care about you, are these words enough to enable you to persevere and not give up?

Read the following scriptures that tell us what we are to be doing, and/or what can help us persevere. Think about, and discuss with others, how you can best experience these things. In Jude 1:20-21, 24, what are we to do, what helps us, and how can we experience these things in our lives? Read 2 Corinthians 1:8-11. What helped Paul persevere and overcome his burdens, and how can we experience the same kind of help? In Romans 8:31-39, what oppositions come against him? What things enable him to persevere and overcome them? What convinces him that nothing can separate him from God's plan for his life? The Bible says that love endures all things (1 Corinthians 13:7). Regarding God's love how is what 1 John 4:16 tells us to do able to help us persevere? According to Hebrews 3:12-14, what do we need that helps us persevere?

In First Samuel 30:6, we read that David, although greatly distressed, "strengthened himself in the Lord". What is needed for a person to be able to strengthen him or herself in the Lord? Perhaps what David says in Psalm 23 is one way he was able to strengthen himself? What in this Psalm can strengthen us? Review this chapter. Find at least six things that can strengthen us and enable us to persevere. Tell how.

PERSEVERANCE

Is it possible to maintain inner peace in our lives in the midst of trials? How do these verses help us have a peace that enables perseverance? (Philippians 4:6-7; Hebrews 4:16; Psalm 73:25-28; Isaiah 30:15.)

ABOUT THE AUTHOR

Originally from Ohio, Jay R. Ashbaucher earned an undergraduate degree in education and a master of divinity degree before serving forty-four years in Montana as a pastor and Bible teacher. He served twenty years as a fifth step counselor and lecturer in an alcohol and drug treatment center where he listened to countless stories of people's broken lives and struggles to achieve wholeness. From them he learned much about people and himself, which has helped in counseling individuals from all walks of life. He has enjoyed conducting grief classes, small groups, and teaching Philosophy of Christianity at a one-year wilderness Bible college. Now retired, Jay continues his Bible teaching as an author, and together with his wife of over fifty years, is enjoying life with family and grand-kids.

AUTHOR'S WEBSITE: https://jay-ashbaucher.com

OTHER BOOKS BY THE AUTHOR

Out of Darkness into the Light: Learning to See Life from God's Point of View–ISBN: 978-1-5136-2878-3

Upload Your Faith Series

The Power of Life-Giving Hope in Troublesome Times (Book-1)–ISBN: 978-1-61314-412-1

Faith: When the Son of Man Comes, Will He Find Faith on the Earth? (Book-2)–ISBN: 978-1-61314-487-9

www.ingramcontent.com/pod-product-compliance
Lightning Source LLC
Chambersburg PA
CBHW071036080526
44587CB00015B/2643